Who Rang the Bell?

by Sydnie Meltzer Kleinhenz
illustrated by George Ulrich

Scott Foresman

Editorial Offices: Glenview, Illinois • New York, New York
Sales Offices: Reading, Massachusetts • Duluth, Georgia
Glenview, Illinois • Carrollton, Texas • Menlo Park, California

Ray is our pet.
He does not stay in the tank.
He may walk all over.

The kids go out to paint.
Vail makes a mess.
He'll go in to clean up.

Vail can hear the fire bell!
It may mean there's a fire.
Vail runs out.

Mr. Bails runs out.

"There is no fire," he says.

"Who rang the bell?" asks Mrs. Fay.

"I don't know," says Mr. Bails.

"Who rang the bell?" the kids ask.
"We have been out all day," says May.
"What is going on?" they ask.

The kids go in.
Ray sits on a desk.
He wants to get some sun.

The kids go out the next day.
Jay needs a pail for sand.
Mrs. Fay lets Jay get it.
Jay hears the fire bell!

Mr. Bails runs outside.
"There is no fire," he says.
"Who rang the bell?" asks Jay.
"I don't know!" says Mr. Bails.

"Who rang the bell?" the kids ask.

"We have been out all day," says Mary.

"No one was inside," says Vail.

"What is going on?" they ask.

The kids feed the birds
They need more seeds.
Faith gets them from the desk.
Faith hears the fire bell!

"Wait!" yells Faith.

"Ray went up when we went out.

He made the bell ring!"

Phonics for Families: This book features words with the *ai* and *ay* spellings for long *a*, and contractions, such as *there's* and *it's*. It also provides practice reading the high-frequency words *when, from, live, don't,* and *hear.* Read the book with your child. Than have your child say words that rhyme with *Ray.*

Phonics Skills: Long *a* spelled *ai, ay;* Contractions

High-Frequency Words: *live, hear, don't, from, when*